find a place

Original Photography
by VA Rivera

Dedication

For you, if you ...

- ✓ *are too familiar with the weight of the world,*
- ✓ *feel overwhelmed by life's responsibilities (externally applied or self-imposed),*
- ✓ *just need a quick break, a few minutes to feel lighter,*
- ✓ *need some fresh air ... or a walk around the block,*
- ✓ *want to remember who you are,*
  - *to feel your feet tight to the ground,*
  - *to breathe energy into your soul,*
  - *to feel capable again*

THIS BOOK IS FOR YOU

find a place

(A MOMENT OF QUIET REFLECTION)

BY: VA RIVERA

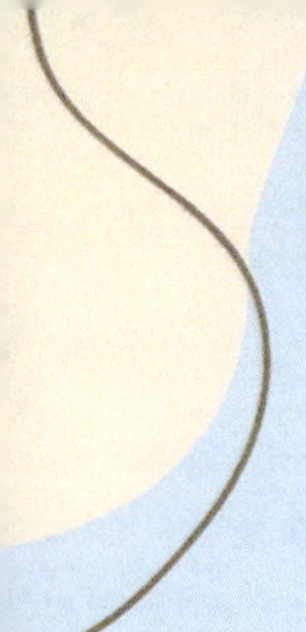

Find A Place

ISBN: 979-8995130611 (hc)
ISBN: 979-8994497999 (sc)
ISBN: 979-8995130604 (e)

The views expressed in this book are solely those of the author and reflect the author's own perspectives and experiences.

VA RIVERA
Poetry Workshops
va_rivera@varivera.com
https://www.varivera.com

Why Find a Place?

Taking time during your day to step back can help maintain focus in day-to-day activities, increase attention, refine clarity, and add to productivity. A daily afternoon break is quite common in many countries around the world.

- Europe's country of Spain carries the tradition of afternoon **siestas** or a ***midday rest*** starting at 2pm for approximately three hours. Italy also has ***riposo*** somewhere between 1 and 4pm, where life purposefully slows down.
- In Greece, **kalomesimeri,** meaning a good midday, is all about escaping the heat and re-energizing. Siesta-like habits called, ***idlip,*** are found in the Philippines, and parts of Mexico and Latin America. Even Nigeria has similar recharge scheduled during each day.

If fitting in a 2 or 3 hour break during your day sounds impossible to you, VA Rivera's pocketbook, ***Find A Place (a moment of quiet reflection),*** is the perfect solution. ***Find A Place*** offers a simple, short remedy for your brain/ body escape whenever or wherever you need ... or want!

S l o w l y read the simple words and phrases. ***L e i s u r e l y*** turn the pages. Imagine yourself wrapped in the illustrated scenes, the meanings of the words, the moments of mindfulness.

You can create your own centered calm in a few moments. You deserve to stop and be kind to yourself- each and every day.

Find A Place (a moment of quiet reflection) offers you a 5 minute re-fresh that can make a difference to the rest of your every day.

SELF-APPLICATION: Some wildflowers (certain buttercups) are designed to withstand freezing, enabling them to bloom early in the spring, often while snow is still on the ground. Flowers can do hard things.

Search in
solitude on
your own,
never lonely,

simply alone.

SELF-APPLICATION: Olive trees are exceptionally resistant, proving dry land and regrowth after floods or harsh conditions. Olive trees embody hope amid adversity.

Pursue peace

of mind,

of spirit,

of heart.

SELF-APPLICATION: Lily Pads release oxygen through photosynthesis during the day to boost pond health and support aquatic life. Lily Pads lift and assist neighbors.

Choose calm

through the storm,

through the

turmoil, towards

the light.

SELF-APPLICATION: Monarch Butterflies' migrate by using a sun-based biological clock combined with magnetic cues. Some 'super generation' Monarchs can store enough fat for a 3,000 mile journey. Monarch Butterflies listen to their bodies.

Like leaves, family

and friends may

change, but

forever remain

the same.

SELF-APPLICATION: Pied Imperial- Pigeons are regarded by some Torres Strait Islanders as the spirits of ancestors watching over the islands from above, representing purity and continuity between generations. Ancestral Family connections are held in highest esteem.

Stand tall,
ground roots
deep.

Steady
perch, plant
firm feet.

SELF-APPLICATION: The Star Lily grows in clusters for vegetative reproduction. Star Lilies strive due to deep roots that store energy for drought, underground seed development, and well-drained soil. Star lilies are deep-rooted not only for development and growth, but survival.

Like stars
that strive
to glow
on darkest days,
unveil pure
radiance every
which way.

SELF-APPLICATION: A single raindrop may take 10 minutes to fall from the rainforest canopy to the forest floor; slowed by the thick layers of leaves, obstacles to its descent. Raindrops in a rainforest take their time.

Footsteps left behind create a trail.

Onward through the wilderness, prevail.

SELF-APPLICATION: The sun's spectrum shifts throughout the day from morning warm reds to midday white to end-day fiery orange embracing each natural phase. Sun's rays are flexible to change and develop, as is required.

Lay upon the
softest ground,
as sun rays
blanket earth's
whispering sound...

until morning
birds abound.

SELF-APPLICATION: Plumerias popular in Hawaiian leis, symbolize positivity, new beginnings, and grace in many cultures. Leis are given as a gesture of welcome, affection, and respect. Leis are an outward symbol of cultural regard, acceptance and honor.

Inhale
verdant aromas

as soft breezes
whisper...

SELF-APPLICATION: A lake's smooth surface will have a mirror-like reflection of the sky and other surroundings only when undisturbed by other elements, such as wind or waves. Lakes best reflect when calm and relaxed.

stay right

here,

place found.

"... Be still, be calm and relax. Then you can reflect on the past, the future, a problem or the path you want to take. So many possibilities limited only by your imagination. Reflections Are Clearest On Still Waters."

- Dave Wagenblatt

Afterthought by VA Rivera:

I was led to ***Dave Wagenblatt's*** perfectly fitting quotation. He writes:

"So many possibilities limited only by your imagination."

Artisit's know the truth of this statement. Educators know. Children inherantly understand the never-ending expanse of their own inventive imaginings.

Every child is born with the gift to create. Reader, that means you, too, no matter your current age. YOU have been gifted with unlimited imagination.

I hope this book helps you tap into that innately-given and precious gift to ***Find A Place*** of peace and calm uniquely your own.

God Bless.

www.ingramcontent.com/pod-product-compliance
Lightning Source LLC
Chambersburg PA
CBRC100831110726
48005CB00011B/1050